SEVEN LUMINOUS PATHS

COLLECTION OF PHILOSOPHICAL POEMS

TOM RUBENS

CONTENTS

"Stimulating and insightful. Take a journey along Rubens' The Seven Luminous Paths, where every poem offers a vista to delight the senses."

My introduction to English literature began in my teens through the reading of quintessential poets like Robert Browning and Lord Byron. As my interests matured, my favoured writer among the Brits became C.S. Lewis. I particularly enjoyed a compilation of Lewis' narrative poems, which still holds a sacred spot on my bookshelf.

The ability to write great poetry is often enhanced by those who have a command of the language in which it is composed. Tom Rubens has taught language and literature for most of his life and written in genres ranging from fiction, to philosophical essays, to poetry. With the publication of *Seven Luminous Paths* his skills and experiences all fuse together to produce an insightful collection.

If I only had two words to describe the poetry selected for this collection, I'd offer these: *effortless / depth*. Meaning, that whether you are new to reading poetry or consider yourself a veteran of the genre, there is an ease to reading Rubens' poems that defies their veiled insights into human nature.

Winter Night on Brixton Road, for example, invites the reader to take a stroll along this thoroughfare on a chilly, wintery evening. After diving into a pub "to spend a penny," we are encouraged through a turn of the poet's thoughts to empathise with the lives of individuals of colour. To contrast their experiences in the present with a darker period in history when many black lives were "Steeped in the static shadows of servitude." It's a timely poem – given the Black Lives Matter movement – and it speaks to Rubens' humanistic sensitivities.

Lovers of the arts will also appreciate the sensual experiences unleashed in Rubens's poems. Stylistically, his verses defy conventional form, yet they curve along with a melodic flow, and are filled with stimulating visuals and evocative words that delight the senses. Consequently, you will not only be enjoying the poem *Penetration*, but you will be buttoning up your coat and feeling its penetrating effects "Like the tip of a slender icicle into flesh . . ."

What's my favourite poem in *Seven Luminous Paths?* That's a tough decision to make. Some poems bring back wonderful memories of childhood, others about romance, and a few delve into thoughts about loneliness and mortality. But if I had to choose one it would be *The Message of*

The Miles. There's an insight contained within its passages – a literary secret of sorts – that thoroughly surprised me.

But I will leave you now, to discover this treasure on your own as well as other thoughtful gems along *The Seven Luminous Paths.*

Scott R. Stahlecker
Author of *Picking Wings Off Butterflies*
and *Blind Guides*
Columnist for *Thinkadelics: The Art of Free thought*

ABOUT THE AUTHOR

 Tom Rubens has been a teacher of English in further and higher education for most of his working life. In addition to the present book, he has published eight books on Philosophy, a selection of poems and three novels. Tom is active in radical politically, and in local community affairs.

THE CORRIDOR OF HISTORY

Tom Rubens

PREFACE TO *SEVEN LUMINOUS PATHS*

This selection of poems has seven theme-sections. They have all grown out of my aim to highlight the fact that areas of experience and observation which are very different from each other can, nevertheless, serve equally as sources of deep illumination and emotional growth. So, the diversity is intended to move the reader to view these areas sympathetically, by being taken to the core of each one—placed right at its centre.

In other words, the theme-groupings are meant to take the reader along a number of distinctive but link-able paths: ones varying in time, terrain, point of focus and emotional yield. Across this spectrum, she will find material on: the historical past, from ancient to relatively recent; the arts, but also the world of nature; intensely personal experiences, plus exploration of public issues; sensuous imagery, as well as ideas and concepts.

The above range shows that the subject-matter has an overall philosophical character. But, at the same time, it is carried on language which unlocks the imagination, and so appeals to all readers of poetry by bringing pictures as clear as can be found in the verse of, for example, a Wordsworth or a Hardy.

Tom Rubens

WATCHING "SPARTACUS"

*The 1960 film, directed by Stanley Kubrick, about the leader
of the failed slave revolt against Roman rule in 70 B.C.
Slavery still exists in some parts of the world.*

Cinemascope with colour and star-names
    Do here for once convey
    some true sense of
    The pastness of the actual past,
    and yet its power
    To burn into the present
    by its difference.

To see:
    Men near-staggering under loads
    They have borne up the same dusty slopes

since puberty,
And edging their way across decades
Of fractured sleep and sickness somehow survived,
Toward complete collapse at some point, then
Disappearance into unmarked holes,
No relative near or knowing.

Or men
Suddenly freed of loads,
And now with adequate food and rest,
But only to be drilled in mind and body
till flung into
Fury of sword or trident lunge:
Blood-shedding hated but compelled,
For sake only of own survival,
And before spectators
Bent on entertainment.

And to see:
Men freed too from this,
For some rebellious, sun-charged hours,
Before the night of reaction's
triumph falls,
And ancient norm of brute oppression
Closes over all its would-be defiers,
As ocean surface does
over dropping ship.

The film, depicting the few
who attempted 'no,'

Brings to mind the remainder,
beyond count,
Who did not, and for whom
No free voice spoke: since,
In that world, submergence of the many

—Multi-pain in permanent shadow—
    Went utterly unexamined, unquestioned.
    Circumstance and attitude were
    mass-burier.

Difference with today is
    Not total but huge enough
    To feel preponderantly,
    As curtain lowers on the screen,
    And audience clap, then stand,
    To walk, each at own pace, through
    open exit doors
    Toward destinations of own choice,
    That power of art has
    Enabled the re-living of
    What has largely been outlived.

DOCKLAND ONCE

The Thames at Rotherhithe: Winter

SUB-ZERO RULES
 At early sink of sun
 Far side of wind-hacked water
 Which here much widens
 from the previous bend.
 Now, in faint bronze light,
 Eye has to
 Strive for satisfaction,
 Deprived of the spires, domes and
 Artistry of sky-line that were
 So abundant further back
 Along the river's
 broad meander.

What stretches before the gaze

Is neither church nor palace nor
Futuristic fuselage of glass and steel,
But instead
A cliff-chain breadth
Of warehouses, grey-brick,
Impressively high but
As mute this waning Sunday
As on each and every Monday.
What were once their windows,
whence ropes swung tautly,
up-hauling merchandise
garnered from across the globe
for just a wealthy few to buy,
Are now, row on row,
Blocked-in squares that
Slowly suggest eye-sockets
bereft of pupils.

No figures hurry at
    buildings' base,
    No growls or laughter carry
    from them to the ear.
    Yet these absences
    Nourish the retina,
    and so the mind.
    And a picture forms: of days
    When warehouse and wharf were
    a-whir with
    Every ounce of strength that
    Sinews could conceivable yield;
    But also when
    scant thought of

The long-term
mingled with the sweat,
Since chief concern was for
The nut-brown flow of tavern beer,
Pennies-priced, toward which
The heavings of afternoon,
Winter and summer, year on year,
Pushed the tiring limbs.

The picture flags,
And mind and eye return to
Now's silent precincts of disuse.
These seem to belong as much
to past
As ramparts of some ancient town.
So too does the toil
Which consumed manhood
and mindhood,
And which, sometimes painfully,
sometimes joyfully, and sometimes
just mechanically,
Made the daily vista of
Hundreds
now beyond trace.

The realisation comes that
These numbers burgeon to myriads,
The farther back, and wider across,
The historical probe extends.
From present vantage point of
Education, opportunity, security

And power to reflect and compare,
The fact that past generations were
Purblindly steeped in perspiration
Looms all the more as being
utterly beyond amend.

BRANDT'S CANCER

Written following the death from cancer of Willy Brandt,
opponent of Nazism and former German Chancellor.

The sweat the swastika's sway
    Enraged him to
    Seeped doggedly through
    Resistance years in Germany
    and in Norwegian exile.
    Yet this rich liquid,
    Like later dedication
    subsuming self,
    Could not by its quality
    Block entry of something
    Much different from the fear
    of liquidation
    long since debarred.

In silence, the walls of the moral citadel
    Were pierced by a process unwinding blindly
    Across tenebrous outer terrain

devoid of human face or sound.
Once past the walls, the penetrator
Swarmed painless through all compartments.
So was shown that spaces
Beyond our high and sturdy handiwork
Should never be discounted, no matter
How obscure compared with
The crystal lights of towers and domes.
They always spread huge in shadow
Outside illumined limits,
Seething incessantly
like a snake heap.
Their turmoil twists all ways,
And sometimes toward and through
our edifices of order:

From whose ramparts
We look out, alert, and scan,
And re-assess fortifications.
The eye does not soften till it turns
away and back
To the familiar pillars and columns,
Each topped by a hewn,
enduring face,
And to the children
playing at their base.

WINTER NIGHT ON BRIXTON ROAD

My overcoat had to be
    Buttoned right to the top even as,
    In the metro's exit hall, I passed beneath
    the ceiling's fluorescent glare,
    Heading for the lesser light of the street.

Outside, the wide pavements both sides
    Were tinged with pale amber
    Shed from glass pods high up
    On stone poles in the biting
    November wind.
    Along the asphalt was continuous movement of
    Figures single and in groups, young to old.
    I slipped into the flow of faces,
    Negroid mainly, purring out, like mine,
    Short steamings as they neared
    Cut-price and bargain stores, late-closing,
    emptying and filling.
    The faces edged forward less slowly than
    The congested cars which skirted them.

Among the cluster were many
Mothers wheeling prams festooned with
Children whose pink or beige or orange
Winter hoods set off,
even under lamplight,
The spectrum of facial browns.

Then, turning into a pub's
Sudden density of light,
to spend a penny,
I saw at the bar a raddled
But grinning ebony face, crowned
with a cream-coloured stetson;
Plus, at a corner table, two big-shouldered
Women of middle age, skin literally black,
Leant toward each other in gossip.

Out in the cold again,
I found my thoughts tracing
a familiar track:
The contrast between the freely unfolding
kaleidoscope of the present
And the past, steeped in the static shadows
of servitude.
But the questions straightaway came:
Was this track simplistic? Was I
Forcing far-ranging facts into narrow corners
of sentimental generalisation?
Did not difference obtain, as with all
large groups,
Between the mean-minded and the generous,
The blinkered and the luminous?
Were there not gaps between individuals

Hard or impossible to bridge?

These questions fomented others,
    so unveiling
    A vista of open country beyond
    the stockades of past oppression,
    A view of enormous spaces whose
    Meandering, even bewildering paths
    All the free must tread:
    Including these,
    threshed by gusts
    of Northern hemisphere
    So different from the African skies
    under which their ancestors were bought,
    And so different from the American skies
    under which they were sold.
    The density of present-tense was unbudging.

In a break in the crowd,
    I saw a figure whose head,
    Bigger than a child's, came only
    As high as most people's waists.
    Its woollen hair was sparse around
    the crown,
    And the man, alone, took slower steps
    than those on either side.
    His eyes were on the flagstones ahead.
    He went by a tall young woman
    standing in a doorway,
    Whose woollen hair was piled, flecked
    with yellow brooches,
    And whose ears sported spangles of blue.
    As he passed, she made a quick eye-motion

Down to him, then an even quicker one
In the direction she'd been looking:
Perhaps, I thought, awaiting her date
for tonight.
The man, not seeing her fraction of a glance,
Kept on forward till he turned into
An unlit, uphill side-street; then
was lost from view.

I could not know for sure
    The thoughts the glance contained,
    Or the kind of space-under-roof
    the man returned to;
    But, from experience where
    faces were mainly white,
    Seeped an informed and cheerless guess.

WHAT WE FASHION

THE FREIZE AROUND THE BASE
OF THE ALBERT MEMORIAL

Seeing the Memorial from
    a hundred yards,
    The eye is held by all the things
    above the base:
    The mass of mellow gold which
    Quietly comprises the seated Prince;
    And the golden frame around him
    Which, in tiers, tapers upward to
    The Gothic apex gleaming
    high over the royal head.

But, from thirty yards onward,
    The gaze divides between this
    vertical shining
    And the grey marble which
    Enfolds beneath it, anchoring it
    to earth.

Though the eye rose
with the golden motif,
With the marble it slowly edges across,
As along a line of choicest verse.
For here it is regaled with
A chiselled vista of life-size figures
Come from every point on
history's compass;
In company together
just this once,
Close-packed, one beside or behind
the other,
Their differences in context dissolved
Into a present-tense they all inhale.
In each figure, unflagging precision
Permeates face, physique and attire,
So that each seems able to step out
From its stone moorings but
chooses not to,
Opting instead to persist in
The nearness which never
threatens identity.
And though each hardly needs
to be named,
Names are attached,
in small bronze letters.
These the eye catches in passing,
As it scans the larger alphabet
Of countenances and postures which
Spell zeniths of attainment
in every major art.

Such convergence in marble

Hints the subtle thunder and roar
of forging-power
Which rolled through each being,
Here shown in mineral silence.
So, silence is echo, of seed-filled winds
Which ravished rare breasts in ways
Onlookers can only try to picture.
Finally,
not onlookers were
The holders of the chisels
That first incised the block of stone,
Then cut paths to free it
from anonymity.

ST. PAUL'S AT SUMMER'S PEAK

Slow curve of far-up ring of pillars
    at daring-chiselled verge of sky
    Gleams chalk-cliff-white in
    Light with power of transparent flame.
    This acute lucency clasps
    Even the slate-grey blue of
    Dome's slope upward from the pillars
    and dizzying inward turn,
    Sheening it as it would
    pavement corundum.

So too are walls' sculpted echelons
    Drenched in noon-stream and,
    At their base, across garden railings,
    The crimson of the rose-whorls

festooning pale-green bushes
is velvet deep.

Inside the garden, sun's otherwise
    Seamless rule is in spots
    Broken by dark-green shafts,
    but still
    Holds a direct line to the head
    Of the golden figure, nine feet high,
    Simply garbed and crook-bearing,
    Whose pate is molten
    And whose presence here
    inevitable.

RIPOSTES

First light may mature to
 Haze of drizzle grey, or pale blue
 Lakes within snow, or blazing indigo;
 Whatever, each evolution of tones
 from dawn on
 Is so remote from our intents that,
 To it, we make riposte,
 Precisely since we know
 those spectra unfold
 not for our response.

Our answer is sometimes sky-level.
 Planes ply unheeding spaces,
 To bring faces and voices together;
 And, high up in the clear blank blue,
 Speak this purpose
 In gleaming, lengthening
 diagonals of white.

At ground-level, replies

Are many. One is
The chiselled in-scape along the frieze
Of walls centuries-standing,
Showing assemblage of figures
three-deep, each distinct
In garment, posture, and insignia held:
So stating how that society saw itself,
And what it wished to affirm
to spectators across time.

Another is
The octave avenues of symphony
and fugue:
The harmony-paths which radiate from
Marriage of mind, touch and instrument,
And which spread skyward, like leaves
in up-wind,
Scattering high and generous
the expressiveness
That will find no counterpart
where it goes.

A third riposte is
The filling of the empty page
With words unevasive and hard-won:
Which inch forward in vital spareness
Till the completed sheet has
The rose-glow
approaching that suffusing
Antique manuscripts
for their import famed.

These and other articulations,

Since meant to reap response,
Define themselves against
The far larger motions of the sky,
Which unravel in
cross-ways free-fall,
Without intention to be watched.

THAMES VALLEY: NIGHT

The view from Noak Hill, Havering, Essex.

At mid-day, the valley is
    Serried land-levels, watercolour
    Shades of difference: grey-blue in sun haze,
    The far-off seeming somehow not so.
    But under black,
    Distance fully declares itself
    In plethora of points of light—
    Pale amber, emerald and red—
    Which range crosswards and outwards,
    Like a hundred Heathrow runways linked.

Each light is tremulous-continuous,
    Faintly pulsating across the miles
    Between it and retina receiving it;
    Fragile, but holding its own,
    And more: for at moments
    The delicacy of its rays

brings to mind
The shine of time-far Christmas tinsel,
Which held young eyes in ways
it cannot older.
And, though vision changes,
What still links child's to adult's
Is the fecund sense of promise
always felt at
Such stellar spread as this
of electric sequins,
Such plenitude man-woven
across the dark.
This array unfailingly
Braces the breast for whatever
Length of future lies ahead.

THE SILENT ORCHESTRA

There is
About wrought stonework at great height,
About hewn leafery, carved gesture of limb
and profiles in frieze
—Seen always at far, fixed edge of
sky's unceasing drift—
A kind of violin note,
subtle, subdued.
The same is so
Of spires expertly honed
to near non-resistance of wind;
And, lower down, of

The perfect verticals by which
Marble pillars rise
to their acanthus crowns.
So too of
The wide, long route
whose sheer straightness
Compels the eye toward the distant
Palace, like a shaded diadem,
placed mid-point at its end.

The delicate string-timbre
    Also sounds from the magnitude of
    Domed auditoria
    boldly circular;
    But equally from
    Concentration of close-knit
    Statuary garlanding a plinth
    With life-size replicas of those
    Whose names echo without limit;
    And, finally, beyond stone's sphere,
    From iron's dance of twirl and line
    In repertoire of design
    inscribed across tall gates.

This choice terrain
    Is a whisper from an orchestra
    Which, in otherwise total silence,
    Plays with power like that of
    Gusts battening mountains
    and churning seas
    In free-wheeling joy at themselves.
    Soundlessly, the orchestra

Pushes every instrument to its
utmost articulation:
Then, to our ears, hints at itself
Along a groove
perception has finely cut.

POETRY GROUP

Weekly we come, each by a different road,
    To the quiet, side-street slope
    And, near its top, the part-open door of the
    Long, narrow room where those already there
    Look round: some with greeting, all with
    A need for unforeseen paths of words.

Each of us carries through the door
    and to a vacant seat
    An inner landscape which we always
    Bear with care along the stone of
    Sunday-silent streets and beneath
    The dim, same-amber glow of lamp-pods
    high overhead.
    This landscape is offered only now.
    Its hills, valleys, plains and spread-out
    Standing figures
    have been fashioned
    From the throng of shapeless daily events
    —from our unique vibrations to them.

So now, having drawn our words out of
This land as patiently as one would
water from deep wells,
We lift them to public hearing in hope
they may be shared,
While knowing their source cannot.

Such understanding of self, so of others,
Pervades the way we both recite
And listen, reveal ourselves or receive
others' revelations.
No wish is felt, or effort made,
To invade other places of origin.
Territorial integrity is by all
Respected, each seeing that
Alternative regions are beyond
Not only access but,
even were that possible,
Also use.

FINALITY

To have contributed is solace
    Enough. Having sunk a portion
    of self
    Into the human-tissued edifice
    Of basic and distinct expression
    Is sufficient cause for calm at
    approach of sleep.
    Provided, while there was time
    and room,
    The inner surges from childhood on
    Were not denied but harnessed
    And perceptively allowed to lead,
    Close of eyes will finalise
    Self's diffusion into
    That plural structure which,
    To individual effort, is
    frieze to single profile.

POWERS BEYOND OURS

DAY'S PIPING

Sky's dense cold grey,
    dawn-born,
    Fissures,
    and lacunae of pale blue
    Let through some few
    January shafts of early sun.
    These slightly brighten
    The thick, bare boughs
    Whose surfaces
    wind scours,
    And etch faint shadows
    beneath them.

Above the inter-knit of branches,
    And across alternation of blue and grey,
    Birds unfailingly ply their way,
    Just as they have night-long.

Through the same breaches overhead,
Sun's rays gain a touch
more strength,
Sharpening the contour of the
Distant slope, so that
Apexed house-roofs, ranged
in upward line,
Show some slate-shine.
Beneath them persists much sleep
soon to expire.

Within an hour,
While wind hums on,
Lake's thinly solid surface
Has partly melted, and on remainder
Prance ducks and gulls,
so conveniently light,
In bold and cavalier denial of cold.
Another hour on, and
Early risers of different ages,
Buttoned high, gather and talk,
Their eager flow of words ensuring
Stream of vapour breath
Amid the still audible moan
that fills the open.
Overhead, blue remains
Fragmentary, lacking tenure sure;
But more people come,
To add their voices to those
whose medium is water or sky,
And to show, as only they
consciously can,

That just a few of the notes
Which day may sound
Suffice to pipe them
Along the path of affirmation.

BELOW SNOWDON

We couldn't see the whole way up
    The three
    far walls of bluish grey
    because of clinging cloud,
    So had to try and guess the highest peak,
    Till someone on our slowly rising track,
    Over-hearing, informed:
    "Snowdon's in the middle."

And on we paced, along
    Earth near-smooth and always
    edging upwards
    Between gradients of green
    That steadily steepened, hinting
    harsher trekking ahead.

This came
    After we'd dipped into the
    Brief respite of flat terrain which
    Vesselled a pale-blue lake

and soothing water breezes.
Came
as we rose
Much higher than before, our feet
Now besieged by jutting rock-lets
On a new kind of track, one
Seemingly hewn in hostility to
the half-hearted.
But, despite the sudden need to
Navigate each new step,
Our eyes often lifted to
Those distant walls which drew
Us on by growing taller,
their summits still obscured.

After much slow and wearying
Steerage of stride, sweat
Lay on our necks and backs,
But cooled quickly in the wind.
To our left, we spied
A lake a half-mile down,
Longer than the one before:
A sinuous interval in hardness of stone,
Its water rendered sea-green
By distance and the surrounding
grass escarpments.
Toward it plummeted
Gulls of spotless white,
As they would toward the ocean,
Being strangely busy this far inland.

Then we looked along and up,
To the middle wall. It was

Higher still, though now,
Through the bluish grey,
streaks of green appeared:
Signs of appreciable nearness, but
These, our legs now told us,
Would not now increase.
So we accepted
staying below Snowdon.
Yet savoured the nether spaces:
The mineral echelons,
aeons-sculpted,
Which fell away
beneath this below.

SOUTH DOWNS

The silence of
    Hamlet streets, and levels of
    Piled hay in barns, and static
    Platoons of rolled-wheat cylinders
    spread across tawny fields,
    Seems exceeded by
    That of the Downs summit.
    Its gaunt contour, neighbour
    for miles to fluid sky,
    Suggests, as we all look up, a final
    Authority in soundlessness.

This impression holds
    In the early stages of our stride-climb
    Up the long escarpment of
    pale green grass.
    But, as lung-lift
    heavies, thigh-muscles tighten,
    And wetness spreads across the back,
    We reach high enough to hear the first

Tentative moan of wind, which loudens,
The more we strain with waning strength
from one tuft to the one above.

At top at last, our foreheads dripping,
    We are wrapped in wind's now
    steady drone,
    And wonder how we ever thought
    Otherwise of this altitude,
    As we quickly don extra clothes
    To halt the coldening of our sweat.

Before us, the horizon
    we'd briefly glimpsed in glancing
    backward while ascending,
    Is now far up, with many
    Squares of field compressed to streaks
    Which form a single surface:
    Linoleum flat, silvered in parts by sun,
    Its smoothness going into mist.

For nearly an hour we savour
    The hum of height and its vantage,
    as we eat and drink.
    Then begin descent. The trek down
    Is easeful, slow, the eye vista-filled,
    And ear by degree freed from wind-cling.
    Sights further down can be leisurely
    imbibed in detail:
    The brown and black flecks of
    Cattle scattered across a grazing basin;
    A combine harvester's centimetres'
    Progress through yellow thickness of corn.

To far left of this mute motion stands
Another Downs summit, seemingly
Presiding over the work below;
and though
As bulky as clustered urban heights,
It assures no need for haste, since
Tomorrow, Monday, will require
no quicker pace than today.

SOUTH DOWNS (2)

Turns of head backward showed
    That each thigh-straining stride
    up the long escarpment
    Was slowly lifting blue-tinged fields
    Towards sky's sapphire, April-fresh.

Escarpment topped, field-rise
    now stopped.
    Ahead spread gradual gradients
    Of pale green or brown toward
    Wide, bare, faintly differing horizons,
    prairie-like;
    But cut, here and there, by small trees
    Whose branches curved leftward,
    from persisting push of wind.

Near our path were head-drooped horses,
    Their Vandyke brown made pristine
    by play of sunlight.
    Either side, ground plunged to swathes

Of grazing land, where sheep were scurf-dots
Casting tiny shadows; as did
A line of tree-lets, their arms
again wind-groomed.
Also below, stretched sheets of
Empty, furrowed soil, grey or beige,
Their breadth breath-catching.

Slow-arced horizons were now reached;
   Then these lowered, to evince
   a vista
   Of small plateaux: now more green
   than blue
   In sun's noon-nearing shine;
   Of different heights; the foreground ones
   With woods in shadowed troughs;
   The slope of one dropping as
   another rose,
   In miniature hint of Highland grandeur.
   And beyond them—the sea,
   Unseen, but inferred from
   A slight-gleaming patch of white
   Nestled on a green contour:
   "The funnel of the Newhaven Ferry,"
   One of our group informed us.

THE SEA AT MARAZION

Marazion is a small town on the southern coast of Cornwall, near Penzance.

The slow drop of the bus
    from the dusty white road
    Toward the plain of sea
    suffused with mid-day sunlight
    Lowers the near-mauve of the water's horizon
    And shows more and more of rippling hues:
    Blues, cream-light or indigo or ultra-marine,
    And greens turquoise or aspidistra-dark
    —All in faintly shifting mosaic across the bay.

The huge flatness of flowing
    coloured glass
    Sports countless fleeting points of
    pin-sharp light.
    At its border, the strong yellow
    Sand widens inward, but also
    Lengthens, and the black flecks

Of people along it thicken.

At beach level, out of bus
    And onto dunes, the eye is
    Lulled by the pale transparency
    Of the shallows at edge of
    beach and rock.
    There is almost a wish that
    This delicate clearness could
    Replace the iridescent sheens
    opaque and further out.
    But the thought passes as
    Eye arcs over total spectrum.

Later, high up once more,
    Out in the bay and looking west,
    From the walls of the castle of
    St. Michael Mount,
    You see how sea-line's height
    exceeds that previous;
    Near-mauve is now near-silver,
    As sun weighs the heavier on
    the greater distance.
    Horizon implies, for the first time,
    The thousands of miles to which
    It is a prelude: those miles
    Whose sequence of undulations
    Will be broken only
    at Indies West.

EARTH'S SEA AND SKY'S SEA

Earth's sea always
    Has an edge we drop our eyes to,
    One with a share of sand, or shingle or rock,
    Somewhere on the giant global curve
    Which wave-turmoil clings to.

But sky's sea is unlike Earth's.
    We must crane our necks
    To follow its upward, boundless spread
    From roof or hill or peak,
    Or at least raise our eyes when it
    Starts from coast or level plain.

Also unlike Earth's is its
    Blue that navigators move
    Through, not on, enclosed in
    windowed shafts of steel.
    And this blue has white packs
    Of not ice but vapour:
    Antarctic cliffs of airy snow,

Or gleaming polar plateaux
—All in indefinite drift.

Sky's sea is more
    Amorphous and more free than Earth's,
    Not planet-gripped; and can quickly
    Fashion, then blur and dissolve,
    Its white islands and peninsulas,
    As if in permanent experiment.
    And it is a sea we
    Must enter with artifice,
    Technics, never simply
    Naked, our limbs our sole support.

Earth's sea is where we
    can be buried,
    In coffins which will fall
    A certain space, then rest.
    But sky's sea has no funereal role,
    No bedrock to receive
    Oaken boxes, or hulls and masts
    Which also mark our once-existence.
    Though sky may seem at times
    the place
    Whose massive motion is fitting
    to absorb us,
    It can no ceremony host,
    no record house.

PENETRATION

It penetrates
    From different angles, different times:
    At grey, wind-gripped noons when
    Bared fingers strain to bend,
    As gusts scour clean the corner-joins
    Of pavement and wall with random
    raging thoroughness;
    Also in milder cold,
    Along sun-hubbed hours of total blue,
    When gold tinges towers of white wide stone
    In a silence persistent yet unimposing–
    An almost-absence at the edge of awareness.

Penetration comes too
    At close of winter evenings a degree more drawn-out,
    As opal dapples of day linger
    High above the diffusing dark, and seem
    A significance to reach for, till their light
    Proves at last expressionless, and fades.

The penetrating
    is not confined to rigours of cold;
    Is felt when the nude, still body
    Sweats beneath the moon, in heat
    Unyielding-mute: like that of August sun,
    Whose molten diaphragm-ing
    Pumps harsh brilliance to the watching, wavering eye.

In all temperatures,
    The realisation enters and sinks,
    Like the tip of a slender icicle into flesh:
    The discovery that sky's variations
    Voice nothing; are massive non-utterance,
    Below which we,
    in our minuteness, speak.

Yet our words, though not far-carrying,
    Are radical sound, our pauses special silence,
    Against the data overhead, and over which
    We hold no rein. Our contrast to
    Wordless immensity is no riposte to it,
    Since of course it has not spoken,
    But is something only we can know:
    A distinction to be nurtured unobserved.

THE WORTHY GOAL

At last,
    Nothing blocks the run of air
    From you through to
    The cumulus plenitude
    against the blue:
    A gathering, at farthest point of sight,
    Like a numberless fleet of
    mythical ships of white.

To this place,
    Immeasurably more than the space
    your two feet have always filled,
    A path is finally clear,
    Since now the self-sheltering
    wall of fear
    Has fallen, banishing shadow
    and the barriers to flow
    of sun-shot breeze and wind.

On these currents

You can now be carried,
Not careless of self but seeing
Self as only part, not whole,
As you make for
the riches of
That far, eye-calling range of fleece
Which is no less worthy a goal
For being
always back-dropped by blue.

EARLY YEARS

PRE-SCHOOL

From the small swings-space beyond
    The greenery below my open window
    Waft the fragile bird-tones of those
    Yet to exchange this week-day
    mid morning surround of silence
    For din of different-darting playground crowds.

As their mothers chat
    with watchful, side-glance care,
    They trace slight arcs through air,
    Or rotate in repeated circles, or
    Thresh legs in sudden spurts of running;
    All the while, with full-faint voice,
    Declaring tiny worlds of self-expression
    Separate from the enormous space around.

· · ·

Though the distance from their mouths to me
    Is short, the air-vibrations feel
    Come from a long way off,
    Their passage honing their distinctness.
    This, I know, is because they are
    Impacting anew on ears which,
    for years too many to count,

Were beyond their echo, immersed
    By daily obligation in rumble and roar.
    That commotion commenced on playground asphalt,
    Then sprawled ever outward.
    But, from that decibel-tumult,
    These ears are now free;
    Across twisting and torrential currents,
    A far bank, embowered, has at last been gained;
    And to this, at first strange-seeming place,
    Can delicate timbres now thread their way,
    Any time of any day,
    creating re-acquaintance.

Yet a question looms:
    When, from first school-steps on,
    Will those of soft-skinned throats,
    The founts of now's so intricate notes,
    Themselves be kissed by needed
    calm like this?

WATCHING 'LOS OLVIDADOS'

*A 1950 Mexican feature film about delinquency and
poverty, directed by* Luis Buñuel.

The heavy black and glaring white
    Of monochrome nearly 60 years old
    Still emits the naked quickness
    in shout and sprint
    Of school-less boys and youths:
    Miniature lords of unpaved, dusty
    and low-roofed streets,
    Far from the city's opulent, hazy towers.
    Also from the celluloid
    Teems the heat of Mexican noon
    and night,
    Continuously gripping the maze of
    Fissured house-walls and makeshift
    doors and fences.

Beneath sub-tropical sky,
    The young are encaved

In urban hinterland which
Induces raw whim to
strike and grasp,
And stifles thought of what
May lie beyond the current minutes.

Almost encaved are we too,
    The viewers plushly seated;
    Almost but not quite, since we
    inevitably ponder
    The twisting of the vitality
    we see depicted:
    The muddying of the streamlet,
    The encrusting of the petal:
    All—again—of 60 years ago.

What now of the depicted?
    If still alive,
    Have they since turned white
    and menial-bowed
    In the same simmering-twilit tract
    Which is Third-World-perennial,
    Knowing no difference
    between decades?
    Were they, therefore, no more
    Than a ripple of groping youngness
    Starting at the edge of vast, still water,
    In which it was bound to fade?
    And were they followed by
    Many more such ripples,
    destined for the same submergence?
    What records are there now,
    Or have ever been, to furnish answer?

And, finally, what of the depicters?
    The raven-hued shocks of hair
    Of the child actors will now be
    Only a little less the tint of snow
    Than those of the teen performers,
    Even if all have always been
    Lucky enough to live far from
    The open prison of penury
    Whose inmates
    they portrayed so well.

WATCHING CHILDREN PLAY

The see-saw rises, and small legs astride it
    Lift with laughter. On the chute of the meandering
    Helter-skelter is a figure in intent descent,
    Arms tucked in for extra glide, and eyes
    Opening and closing. On the swings, some
    Scale higher than others, with skilful turns
    of waist and neck.
    In the sand-pit, explorers waddle
    Backwards and forwards, flushed faces
    powdered yellow.

All are deeply immersed, swimming
    The impulses of a present-tense which for them
    Is utterly un-moored,
    unconnected, but,
    For the onlooker, not.
    S/he stands and gazes
    On ground bound to a past from which
    It cannot float free to an open-ness of future:
    A past cut with trench-lines of struggle,

failure and success
That also span the present, and point ahead
One way and not another.

The unreined spontaneity of the playground,
        Its winning venture in simple movement,
        Knows as yet nothing of the markings
        Which cannot be veered from. They make
        Different paths for those long past
        The sameness of elementary triumph with
        Skipping rope, ball, plasticine and pencil;
        Also long past mastery of kinds
        more complex
        though not distinctive.
        The distance now is such that
        Distinction is known to be
        Clasped or out of reach: the fact
        Which parts paths the widest,
        interposes a mountain range,
        decreeing
        Whose sweat and joy will be
        the common heritage, and whose not.
        The verdict may seem harsh,
        Denying most a niche in the public future;
        And to wake each day to this decision
        Pleasures not those of erstwhile hope.

Yet,
        to see what rides the waves
        Of generations, the crest-foam that endures,
        Is in fact
        to be carried along just beneath
        that rarest white.

Though not the carrier, the perceiver
Participates in a general way, one
Which hopefully awaits
many whose present,
Easy and past-less mirth
the adult eye defines.

FILM POSTERS

The big square sheets pasted
 Strategically on street corners
 No longer hold the eye
 With the command they once did.
 The clustering of different
 Face-angles and word-sizes,
 In seemingly ever-new schemes
 of colour,
 Has lost its old absolute authority.
 The compressed coil of images
 not seen before
 Now fails to spring out at you
 With its former irresistible force.

Before, the worlds the rectangles
 etched
 Appeared more real, more worthy
 of attention,
 Than anything that might be happening
 On the bustling pavement where

You would, each Monday, stand
Dependent and agape
At another fresh offering, another
Successful intensification.
All that then mattered was those
Few square feet, bordered
by wall-brick,
But building in your mind
To an area wider, higher, longer
Than anything touchable
around them.

So why the difference now?
    One reason is that
    The spaces beyond the posters
    Have grown clearer, their detail
    sharper,
    And are not now the mere
    Bright blur they were
    To the young, unpractised eye.
    Those spaces too have meant stories,
    Have taken you along their paths,
    And expanded till their sheer breadth
    Can scarcely be traversed:
    Till, indeed, they have outbid all else
    for your comprehension.
    The roll and wash of
    free-flowing distances
    Over the posters have
    effaced their centrality.

And so have shown that
    The total control over events

Which the poster-pictures portray—
The hold on a beginning, middle
and end—
Belongs only to makers of images:
Those who wield the small power
Of extracting and mastering
Some elements only
From the surrounding
heaving of happening.

The posters' eclipse has
        another reason too.
        Those chiselled and rare profiles
        and expressions,
        That fire in the eyes, that
        vividness of feature—
        All seemed once to be
        Radiantly permanent, declaring that
        Their owners breathed a choice and
        Separate air from ours, one which
        Barred decay, hazard, extinction:
        Gashings which, the years would teach,
        Reach all,
        the winnowed beautiful
        no less than you.

The third reason is that
        Your scale and speed of thought
        Have out-spaced what the poster—subjects
        Called for. The book,
        especially,
        Lengthened your line of mind
        Much beyond the ninety minutes

Which was all the film demanded.
The printed page set you moving through
Paragraphs and stanzas of richly
uncertain number;
Through far more stages of thought
Than any film encloses, and
Across the warp and woof of words,
as intricate as patterns of lace,
Which no film can wholly trace.

Now, therefore,
The posters are no longer the core
Of your mental thrust. They still
Play a part, are still an acuteness,
But only one of many:
The latter bearing emphasis,
Since the open site of so much more
toil of thought to span.

GROUNDS FOR PREDICTION

Summer plethora of clans of
    Peach-smooth boy-faces and
    hairless threshing limbs
    Just eight or nine Junes old,
    Reminds of the equivalent
    Of forty years ago, when days were
    Dinghy-rockable, and ball-bouncing
    Hours on asphalt or grass
    Stretched till evening's red.

These were hours when
    Separate busy mirths
    brushed against each other,
    Mainly self-enjoying, with as yet
    Little to appraise of self and others.
    But, with time, up to and through
    The years when voice-bells cracked
    And chins glinted with first stubble,
    The task of estimation pressed,
    though not on all.

From then, there could be
    No return to the buoyant bustle
    of before,
    As growing differences in action
    Lengthened, like shadows pointing
    many ways,
    And people re-grouped tacitly,
    Each turning inward to
    A certain set of sympathetic faces.
    Some were powerfully drawn
    to define,
    And cast wide description's net;
    Others not, seeking only
    To stay outside the casting.

Discrepancies finally emptied
    The asphalt and grass of that first
    spontaneous mingling.
    They grew even more
    for the few
    Who kept to appraisal's
    steepening slope,
    And rose to where they saw,
    far below,
    Many kinds of persisting motion
    which knew not
    their own banality.

The mind now returns to this summer's
    Boys at unflagging play,
    And makes a certain prediction,
    Without malice, but also
    without a smile.

BY-WAYS OF LOVE

RENOIR'S "THE LUNCHEON PARTY"

Lengthy-oblique, the painting's title
    Is in its way as subtle as
    The brush-strokes of yellow, tawny,
    Pale-green and white which deliver
    the mid-river
    Mild sunshine of an afternoon
    One hundred and thirty summers fled.

Each dab and fleck renders
    Not only era and hour but also
    The angles of the many
    fresh-hued faces
    Across the canvas's archetypal
    Clustering of the hopeful young.

Renders also
    their lines of gaze.
    That the latter all differ; that

No-one looked at is intent on
the looker,
And that all look,
Are the ironic mosaic of points
Which make up
The picture's implied and brief
sub-title,

And also
Much in the mature viewer's
own summers gone.

THE CAFE

Especially in early evening,
When the fawn, cylindrical lamp-shades
Mild-glow across the window's
wide frontage,
You wonder, from a distance,
on vague way to somewhere else,
'Shall I?'
And the recurrent answer 'Yes'
Draws you again to the bell-chimed door.
This, you know, will once more
Open onto the behind-the-counter
Smile which
Is for you
donned and defensive,
And yet which
still unintentionally
Enhances the features you have found

no equal of.

The concealing smile never budges,
    And the large brown eyes hold opaque,
    As you request the
    perfunctory cup of coffee
    That is your passport to
    Proximity for some short while:
    During which you can,
    From a corner table,
    entirely without imposing,
    snatch glimpses
    Of the different facial angles,
    And hear the various,
    Lilts of voice, in the serving
    of each new customer.

For some time you have known
    That she fully saw
    The meaning which your

Eyes let slip one day when
    they couldn't help
    Resting on the delicacy of
    The folds of her diminutive ears,
    beneath dark hair swept back and up
    in high bun.

So you have known that
    The reason for her tautness is
    non-requital;
    But have also known,
    and with a certain gladness,

That the tautness shows
Integrity, and no impulse to cajole.

Yet, clear on all this,
    You still ask your question
    Whenever the cafe is in sight,
    Since you always need
    Still more of the certainty
    The bell-chimed door is path to:
    That you would never seek
    Another face for nearness,
    Did this one but seek it with yours.

ALREADY SPOKEN FOR

"I'm already spoken for,"
    Had been her clear-eyed, sole reply,
    But the lightness of the cliched phrase
    Was not hard-meant, and simply showed
    Where her completely certain focus lay:
    One which he'd sensed then,
    And later knew beyond a doubt,
    could not be changed.

For her, the words had been
    A quick handful scooped
    From the liquid flow of time;
    But, for him, a new current to it,
    Channelling still more days
    Into inventive study of
    The rare gestures and light-of-eye
    Which were hers and which,
    On first seeing, he had discovered
    To be the goals
    of earlier, vaguer search.

Deepening in this direction,
    While she did in another
    which he could not follow,
    He meandered among past years,
    And found her in places she had
    Never been but should have:
    In the school playground when,
    Face peach-smooth and voice unbroken,
    But musing on an older girl
    Of dark and quiet features,
    He had first been moved by
    Woman-dignity, as by
    a ruby on green velvet;
    And later, puberty reached,
    When thoughts first came of
    life-sharing.
    He saw her elsewhere too:
    In the nodal points of promise
    That sparsely gemmed the years,
    When hers and his and
    other separate pairs of eyes
    Lifted to the morning blue
    In exceptional aim and intent.

This ubiquity, he glimpsed,
    Meant that she was part of him.
    This constructing of her was
    How she lived within him--
    How she burgeoned, and would
    continue to,
    In spite of being spoken for.

THE MESSAGE OF THE MILES

The hill-top park, which was full
    this hour in summer,
    Now has only the odd evening walker
    Tinted with tawny light from a sun
    Which stands pale-molten amid cloud,
    Just above the silhouetted tree-line.
    As the orb holds its marginal place
    before disappearing,
    Copses cast long shadows eastward,
    and bright greenness recedes.
    The sky, filling two thirds of the view,
    Is tundra, with ridges of grey and
    lakes of fading blue.
    The wind against the face
    Sweeps stronger across the higher tract.

People are less to be seen than
    Linked with houses that dot the distance;
    Less a presence than an idea—
    One which shapes itself the more distinctly

In those to whom the outstretched miles
Declare: 'You lack a lasting companion.
At no point along our length does
Your shadow merge with another,
Or your body lie down with a second
In union which our cold echoes cannot
pass through.
Without this fusion, there is only
Our far minutiae for your eye
to comb, stopping on none.'

Agreement with these words reminds
That surrounding emptiness has sometimes
Shot racking shudders
through limb and breast, and impressed
That it is the sole alternative to
a genuine sharing of lives—
Which must, then, be the goal.
For not to reach it means
That blue-tinged land-lines are really
No further off than the talking faces
Which roll across the hours between
Lone opening and closing of eyes;
And means
that to none of these visages
Can the eye dilate
And speak the need to lift the weight
of self
From its unshared piece of ground
To one where self turns weightless,
At the touch of a committed hand.

CROWDED DO

At first, it seemed just another
  Noisy London
  New Year's Eve do,
  In a professional someone's house
  To which I'd been invited
  by a friend of friend.
  Faces were close-packed,
  The gaps between them
  Barely enough to put wine-glass to lips,
  Yet criss-crossed with speedy words
  Signalling status and apparent confidence.

Along the side of the food table
  Spread with quiches, cheeses, hams,
  burgundies and spumantis,
  I inched my way, wondering
  How I'd manage conversation,
  Balancing a filled paper-plate in one hand
  While sipping with the other.

For now, I chose food only,
To leave a chance for shaking hands.
My friend of friend introduced me
Round. I followed him as we
Squeezed and slid between pairs of shoulders,
And I smiled from one set of
Astute, pleasure-seeking eyes
to another.

All at once, ahead,
    In a space less narrow,
    Was a face
    in profile, which
    Hurled my mind,
    by reflex,
    Back into wide-openness of the past,
    in search of
    What I sensed was a memory
    to be grasped,
    And then it was.
    'But it couldn't be,' I said
    without words, stopping still.
    "I'll catch you up," I called to friend's friend,
    Who looked back, smiled, moved on.
    'Simply couldn't be,' I added mutely.
    As gaze
    fell along the feminine-bold line of nose,
    And down to tender turn of chin,
    Then rose to forehead's highness,
    And wandered in the hair's honey-gold.

From the person she was talking to,

She slightly turned her head,
to acknowledge someone else's greeting,
Till the profile was restored.
With this, now came to me something like
Certainty, breath-quickening. But to be
Really sure, I turned to someone
next to me,
And asked 'do-you-know-who-that-is?'
"Yes, that's Karen....." The surname
I hardly heard, didn't need to hear,
As I leapt back twenty years
to where,
Surrounded by the silent, near-boundless
Brush land of sub-Saharan tropics,
I had yearned, without issue, for
The features now before me
and only faintly changed.
As was her body: just a shade weightier
Than the elfin-slenderness
of her
Running in slacks and sandals on
scorched, tawny soil,
Or breast-stroking through water
clear as glass.

Other shapes, sudden-profuse,
    Also cancelled the two decades:
    My first sight of her, the new lecturer,
    In the library of the small university
    where I taught,
    And her fleeting, precision-glance
    In my direction as she passed,

hair kerchiefed.
Then, after meeting and talking,
Our coffee-drinking in her bungalow,
In the same corner of the campus as mine;
And my embroidery of hopes,
there being
No ring on a certain finger.
But, after this, her mention of
Husband in England, and my
Silent, invisible wrench-inside,
and in effect withdrawal;
Only to see, later, someone else
Her frequent guest, who,
at staff gatherings,
Spoke with Australian accent and,
When husband came on
unsuspecting visit,
Laughingly clinked glasses with him.

Under the stars of African sky,
I would often hear the stopping
and eventual re-starting
Of the lover's car, as I
Waited till time to sleep
To muster strength for one more
unshared, sweat-damp, working day.
And, as these days built into months, I saw
That lover might well replace husband
For her for whom I longed no less.
This was as much as I could see
When, work-contract over, I shook her hand
and smiled in friendship,
And wished her all the best,

Before the cab to airport,
To be on schedule
Swooped upward by huge steel wings
In trajectory beyond reverse.

But irreversible too
    Was that she, though by men
    inevitably much-attended,
    Filled for me a separate space as
    Source of my first ever love-pang.
    So, a face that would in memory
    Mingle with later ones of like impact
    Across the ensuing
    years of isolation.

And her face
    Was now just feet away,
    Dropped into place by some uncanny
    Wing-beat of circumstance
    passing overhead.
    Should I go up to her, or just
    Stay near, anonymous but imbibing?
    Scarcely had the question formed than
    I found myself going forward, with
    "Karen?" On the word, her profile
    Became full-face, the new angles
    Releasing another rush of remembrance.
    "Yes?" was the reply, her blue eyes
    Void of recognition. I swallowed,
    Willing to withdraw with apology
    of some sort.
    But she went on, politely, "Sorry.
    Do I know you?"

Creating a smile, I gave the name of
The university, the dates, then who I was.
Blueness flickered, faintly, and
Oh yes....yes." Then, "What a long time
Ago it was! What are you doing now?"
I said where I was teaching, then returned
The question, adding others.
When she spoke of a new marriage,
in Australia, after leaving Africa,
And return to England with family
several years later,
I recalled my prediction,
And for a moment tried to picture
First-husband's face when, at long distance,
she had delivered her decision.

Throughout her information,
    I glimpsed no sign of
    Thoughts of me along the years,
    No shape of me in the later
    architecture of her mind.
    And when the statements were complete,
    There came a certain awkward silence:
    She had reached the end of
    all she chose to say on the past,
    While from deep disclosure I was
    self-debarred.
    Then her head moved slightly,
    Hinting impulse to talk to someone else.
    I smiled to show 'okay,' and she smiled
    A kind of 'thanks'; then moved a little
    To the left, and was straightaway
    Effervescent with a probable long-term friend.

This, I assumed, resumed
Her main sweep of mental flow,
Which talk with me had diverted briefly.

The distance between us
Was now about the same as when
I had first seen her tonight.
We might talk again, on other things,
In a re-configuring of crowd,
But again it would be
without true upshot.
So, the few feet of separation stood for
the score of years--
Space for time, the small for the large--
And were in essence as
unbridgeable as an ocean.

It would not matter, then, if I moved away.
So I did, unobtrusively,
Between yet more pairs of shoulders,
Till I bumped into friend of friend
Coming the opposite way. He of course
Hoped I was enjoying myself,
To which I nodded, then continued forward,
Toward the pile of coats
in the small room by
The front door. Mine I mined
From near the bottom, then buttoned up
to the neck,
Before turning the door-knob in hope
That no-one would call out,
"What? Going already? It's nowhere near
midnight yet!"

No-one did, and the way was clear for
Unembarrassed exit into the
unpeopled cold,
And the silent, homeward walk, long enough
To ponder an even wider time-expanse than twenty
years.

━━━

END-POINT

TURN AWAY

As the eye, having savoured,
    Can turn away
    From the long table ranged
    With roasts and fruits and claret glass,
    So too it can
    When vigorous noons display
    The plinths, arches and cupolas
    Of accomplishment; when they show,
    In column heights and
    triangle friezes,
    What it was born among
    And will outlast it.

These the eye, while kindled,
    Knows it won't always hold.
    Its route to them, as to

Children's jerky running,
And the precision-ing
of faces into puberty,
And the ripples of movement of
clustered heads that pack a stadium,
Will in the end be cut.

Seeing this fashions restraint.
  Distance-from balances closeness-to,
  Then sinks lower, so that
  Vision is at any time
  Ready to relinquish its objects
  And resist their beckoning;
  Is prepared to move from
  Rich-wincing at gleam of marble array
  To shadow of empty space.

Such motion has nothing bitter.
  It is simply wise rehearsal,
  Action with foresight.
  Acceptance of darkness is not
  rejection of light.

BRUTE SLIDE OF CIRCUMSTANCE

Plunge of boulders or mud-lanche
    Down long wide slopes onto
    Small accretions of match-stick roofs
    Is an image of no-control which
    Near-maddens the vulnerable eye.

So too are:
    The sky-unfolding which parch
    Both soil and throat, leaving
    corpses over cracks;
    The bullet's splicing the infant skull;
    And the screaming freedom of the torturer
    Within his blood-smeared walls.

No control:
    no blocking of lethal sequence,
    no stop on hard, arbitrary sweep;
    no answer, then, to
    the call of the heart.

To see, through eyes
now narrowed and steadfast,
That this absence is constant,
Is to cease all invocation.

UPWARDS WHILE DOWNWARDS

In that inexorable loss of height,
 From eye-wincing white of snow peak
 Down brown slopes in bright but
 weaker light,
 And towards the always sunless
 Lake of shadow at mountain's base,
 We should accept the final dashing
 Into dark, deep water, but
 not inertly.

Though lacking wings to stay descent,
 We may fashion a self-extension
 Which flows backwards, the way we came:
 A spinning of fine-gold strands from
 gestures
 free-fall
 generous.
 The denser the weaving into empty space,
 The higher into sunlight it rises;

Till production must cease,
And strand-work float detached
In upper air, delicate
indestructible.

THE WINDOW

The Window,
    unmisted at summer noon,
    Is so wide,
    so thronged with
    blue and crimson figures
    dotting wheatfield-yellow
    right to the horizon,
    That you may think
    It will always, bountifully,
    as if measurelessly,
    Surround you as now it does.

But not so.
    The huge pane,
    at a tiny point on which
    you are, like a fly, located,
    Will finally show its corner,
    When, with travel of mind and time,
    Your position will have changed.

Then, being at window's
   sharp right-angle,
   you will
   accept;
   seeing less through the glass,
   you will
   acquiesce in.
That light then will lie
   only to one side of you,
   Is a fact you will not evade.

DIFFERENT SCENES, DIFFERENT LIGHTS

WRONG JOB ETC.

To have to be with
    In practice strangers
    For half the waking hours,
    Including when the sun is high,
    Makes sleep-time seem
    Still more subtraction from
    The chance for shared discovery

Which, beyond the window,
    The travelling sky suggests:
    But which, below, at
    coffee-break level,
    Between imitations of activity,
    The token talk, then
    Disappearance, discreetly

kill:

Leaving you the after-work
　　Questions: 'Who are they really?
　　Do they ask the same of me?
　　Are their routines from fear?

And leaving you
　　The grind of headlights along
　　clogged roads,
　　Then the dim-lit climb to
　　second floor,
　　Where, pinned on your
　　foot-marked door,
　　A note says rent is overdue.

⊏　⊐

ENDWARFMENT

Sky's expanse of serried summits and of blue
　　Is now no more mere backdrop to the human face
　　But a frontal vastness dwarfing it.
　　Depth of eye, which once seemed measureless
　　And not bound by bone,
　　now shows itself enclosed
　　Within the skull, within a shape that is
　　Small and fragile against the vapour zone
　　Around and above it. Before, the face's

Animation seemed the naturally
Central thing, but has now receded to
The lower and only edge of boundless air.

ASHEN HAIR LONG AND THICK

A cloudless, mid-summer Saturday,
  And a park-top cafe, into which
  Stream families with push-chairs,
  And teenage clusters, and children
  magnetised by ice-cream signs:
  All queuing, calling, chewing, sitting
  in unwitting statements of togetherness.

A gap in the flow, and then
  Again the woman appears alone:
  Her ashen hair long and thick
  And, as before, in a style vaguely
  1940's;
  Her creased face a leather-brown—
  Meaning many hours beneath
  the hot and silent blue.
  Once more, her eyes glint tension.

In the queue, there are children
  Back and front of her, pointing

"I want" to compliant parents.
Yet her gaze is not on them but on
The wide, high glass of the cafe wall,
And the distances showing through it.
On the tray she now carries to a corner table
Is not the colourful salad or pastries
most people buy
But a cindered version of fish and chips,
Their brown just darker than hers.
Into them she pushes knife and fork,
eyes either down or glass-wards.

Comes the question: Is she childless?
Then: Is she widowed, divorced or spinster?
No finger-rings give clue.
Then: How does she see
the years ahead?
Whatever the answers, they do not project
From that corner table, where lips,
the meal now over,
Are pursed like those of
an unyielding captive.
Whether they will stay so
cannot now be seen,
As, after standing, she turns her body
And trudges past an infant's tricycle,
to the exit and out.

IRON DARK

Slightly and pleasurably winces the eye
    At night streets' neon sheen
    of gaudy red, yellow and green.
    But it also sees above
    this line that shines, like a row of big
    imitation gems, to give quick ease
    at ground-level;

Sees to where the wincing ceases, and eye,
    Now clear of this light, dilates without evasion
    At darkness dense as iron.

Hard black bolts the join between itself
    And the city's glimmering roof:
    Fixes the point above which glows
    cannot rise;
    Without break, fills the opaque
    canopy of space
    Like the inside of a jet stupendous

helmet.

Firm and complete in its
    recurring dominion,
    Darkness slides the lock on hopes
    That only thrive in dance of light.

MONEY

Though not you,
    Digits on a balance sheet
    can seem so.
    The small black figures neatly spaced
    In columns on crisp white paper
    Are nothing like
    the re-discovered
    Faded photos by which you
    Truly return to self
    after long vagaries of doubt;
    But, so keenly do you consistently
    scan those numbers,
    As someone afraid of ageing
    daily scans face in mirror,
    It's as if they really did
    spell identity.
    Though not you, they seem to
    lock to you
    Like a shadow to a solid figure,
    Moving with the latter's

very slightest motion.

Yet, that they are not you
    Is clear when their
    sudden drop
    Brings, not shock but an
    unexpected even breathing,
    Such as lungs would work when
    Just over near-exhaustion.
    This curious composure, kindling hope
    Of its continuance even in moments
    of mortal crisis.
    Speaks solely you: you as you
    sensed yourself
    When first you ran on legs as young
    as plant-shoots,
    Or first wept at causing pain.
    The even-ness declares that
    Digits do not delineate; and that
    The cord between you and them
    Can be cut at any time, at call of
    The blood-quickening task
    Which hurls security aside.

MORE AWARE AND CHASTENED
SELF

To glimpse, far too late,
    How deeply you gashed another's mind,
    How wildly you wielded the psychic knife,
    Leaves you
    afraid of yourself as of a stranger,
    And groping for a way out of
    The dark cavern which has now
    dropped massively around you,
    As complete comprehension of
    the underground of self.
    In the shadows, as trembling fingertips
    comb stone surface,
    And you seek a pocket of light
    that would mean escape,
    You think of the measureless
    thickness of rock
    Blocking off the gentle, generous gestures
    which also comprise your past
    and tell of another you--
    One instinct with morning sunshine

and vistas of blue.
Then, all at once, you see
where the shadows thin,
And toward the faint rays you move
With steadier step; while knowing that
A return to open spaces still leaves
The walled-in ones a fact of
unsparing recollection.
Mind's inmost caves and deepest wells
Stay markers of what once you did:
Recesses never to be reached by
The sun-shot wind of the clearing
Toward which your present,
more aware and chastened self,
aspires absolutely.

THE PERSISTING LINK

Now her Sundays are passed
    With old Bert, a fellow pensioner
    From the local club, a widower
    Who's not badly off and treats her
    To trips to Southend and Brighton;
    " just for the company."

Sunday used to be the day
    She began early in the kitchen
    To prepare the roast that
    Husband and son would sit down to,
    Always a little after one.
    Then, washing-up over, she'd take

Son to the park, or to see
Her mother or brother, and they'd
Talk about what he was doing at school,
Or longest rivers and capital cities.

Photographs of husband, mother
    and brother
    Now stand on the sideboard,
    With many others, and the son,
    On his weekly visits, notes
    That she often re-arranges them.
    He knows he could come
    more often,
    But doesn't, because his mind
    Is now nowhere as close to the
    world of the pictures
    as hers is.
    About that world he mostly listens,
    Nodding, pretending to remember.

And he doesn't like to see
    Her sudden pauses, when memory
    Flags, and her eyes drift to the window
    And the street from which all the old
    Neighbours have gone: moved or died.
    The silences tense him, since they say
    That, in spite of the club and Bert,
    She treads alone, except for himself,
    To whom she must finally turn.

Saying this too are
    The television-sounds,
    like live voices and far too loud,

Which he hears in the background
When he phones to ask
what kind of day she's had.
When he mentions the sounds,
She replies, "Well, you know,
it's company."
'That word again,' he reflects.

He keeps some distance, then,
  And has his own life, about which
  He could tell her more but doesn't.
  But, even with the gap, and
  His unease about ultimate duty,
  He intuits a thread that links them:
  The same as connects us all
  To that nook in the landscape which
  Gave us shape and start,
  and from which
  We cannot cut ourselves, whatever
  the complications.
  Our point of origin fills a unique space,
  As do the kin-figures ranging either side:
  All making a corridor of time
  that bears a family name.

       ⊏⊐

SUNDAY SILENCE

It's at Sunday dawn,
  When entire sky is water-turgid
  Cloud whose heavy grey
  Is just bright enough to tinge

The soaked dark of roofs frail pale,
That the already active ear
Most needs its food, and is
most denied it.

Decibel-absence now
    Is felt more keenly than are
    The lacunae between routine
    weekday clamours,
    Since for this seventh day
    There lingers habitual hope
    Of choicest chimes
    From somewhere far
    past people,
    And bringing, with their vibrations,
    Certainty of unfailing aid
    when need arises.

But, as the waking wait begins
    once more,
    The ear feels again the tonnage
    Of anti-sound, its density granite-like.
    And, this time, from ear-drum inwards,
    There spreads a sense of having to
    Shake off passive expectation,
    Push against the overhanging weight,
    Till the strain creates a groan
    Which, whatever pain it voices,
    Is at least your sound
    and a scoring of the surface of
    silence's rock-face.

The thoughts that such marking

Is maybe the most
to be achieved,
And that stony inner layers are,
this side of them,
impenetrable,
Stifle the erstwhile hope.
It is now replaced by
A need for people-decibels,
Of struggle as of joy,
And by the view that only these
echo the chance of help.

OTHER BOOKS BY TOM RUBENS

Book 1 | Book 2 | Book 3

The Illumination Trilogy

The trilogy does encourage the reader to think histori-
cally about modern Western society: about the differences
between the pre- and post- WW2 contexts, and especially
about the periods when those differences were most
marked. This stimulus is of course additional to the foci on
the intricacies of personal relationships and on general
philosophical ideas—which are the texts' two chief features.

These foci indicate my wish as author to show how
the two things can be intimately linked, when the personal
sphere has access to the public sphere of intellectually
advanced culture. To repeat, that access is possible largely

because the social attitudes and conditions which favour it have wide influence: as they did have in the 1960s and 70s, but as they don't have, to the same extent, in the current period.

Tom Rubens.

Lightning Source UK Ltd.
Milton Keynes UK
UKHW021541250921
391174UK00002B/135